Applying the Standards:
Math
Kindergarten

Credits
Content Editor: Julie George
Copy Editor: Elise Craver, Angela Triplett

Visit *carsondellosa.com* for correlations to Common Core, state, national, and Canadian provincial standards.

Carson-Dellosa Publishing, LLC
PO Box 35665
Greensboro, NC 27425 USA
carsondellosa.com

ISBN 978-1-4838-1565-7
01-005151151

Table of Contents

Introduction

The purpose of this book is to engage students in applying the standards to real-world, higher-level thinking problems. Each Common Core mathematics standard is covered by one or more practice pages.

Students will be expected to answer a few straightforward problems to prove basic understanding of the standard. Then, they are presented with a higher-level thinking problem. These problems are designed to require students to demonstrate their complete understanding and flexibility with the standard. Finally, a reflection question guides students to review their work on the previous problem. The reflection questions are designed to support the Standards for Mathematical Practice as students are asked to study their approaches, their successes, and their struggles.

Use the included rubric to guide assessment of student responses and further plan any necessary remediation. Understanding and applying mathematical knowledge to realistic problems is an invaluable skill that will help students succeed in their school years and beyond.

Common Core Alignment Chart

Use this chart to plan your instruction, practice, or remediation of a specific standard. To do this, first choose your targeted standard; then, find the pages listed on the chart that correlate to the standard.

Common Core State Standards*		Practice Pages
Counting and Cardinality		
Know number names and the count sequence.	K.CC.1– K.CC.3	5–8, 10
Count to tell the number of objects.	K.CC.4, K.CC.5	7–10, 12
Compare numbers.	K.CC.6, K.CC.7	11–16, 21
Operations and Algebraic Thinking		
Understand addition as putting together and adding to, and understand subtraction as taking apart and taking from.	K.OA.1– K.OA.5	9, 17–35
Number and Operations in Base Ten		
Work with numbers 11–19 to gain foundations for place value.	K.NBT.1	36–38
Measurement and Data		
Describe and compare measurable attributes.	K.MD.1, K.MD.2	39–44
Classify objects and count the number of objects in each category.	K.MD.3	45–47
Geometry		
Identify and describe shapes.	K.G.1–K.G.3	48–56
Analyze, compare, create, and compose shapes.	K.G.4–K.G.6	57–62

Problem-Solving Rubric

Use this rubric as a guide to assess students' written work. It can also be offered to students to help them check their work or as a tool to show your scoring.

4

_____ Answers all of the problems correctly

_____ Identifies all of the key numbers and operations in the problem

_____ Uses an appropriate and complete strategy for solving the problem

_____ Skillfully justifies answer and strategy used

_____ Offers insightful reasoning and strong evidence of critical thinking

_____ Provides easy-to-understand, clear, and concise answers

3

_____ Answers most of the problems correctly

_____ Identifies most of the key numbers and operations in the problem

_____ Uses an appropriate but incomplete strategy for solving the problem

_____ Justifies answer and strategy used

_____ Offers sufficient reasoning and evidence of critical thinking

_____ Provides easy-to-understand answers

2

_____ Answers some of the problems correctly

_____ Identifies some of the key numbers and operations in the problem

_____ Uses an inappropriate or unclear strategy for solving the problem

_____ Attempts to justify answer and strategy used

_____ Demonstrates some evidence of critical thinking

_____ Provides answers that are understandable but lack focus

1

_____ Answers most or all of the problems incorrectly

_____ Identifies few or none of the key numbers and operations in the problem

_____ Uses no strategy or plan for solving the problem

_____ Does not justify answer and strategy used

_____ Demonstrates limited or no evidence of critical thinking

_____ Provides answers that are difficult to understand

© Carson-Dellosa · CD-104845 · Applying the Standards: Math

Name _____

Count the objects. Write the number.

1. 🐸🐸🐸 _____

2. 🌸🌸🌸🌸 _____

3. 🐟🐟 _____

Solve. Show your mathematical thinking.

4. How many more fish are needed for a total of 10?

Reflect

How did knowing how to "count on" help you solve problem 4?

_____

_____

_____

_____

Count by tens. Trace each number as you count.

1. 10 ten   20 twenty

    30 thirty   40 forty

    50 fifty   60 sixty

    70 seventy   80 eighty

    90 ninety   100 one hundred

Solve. Show your mathematical thinking.

2. Avery read 2 books. Each book had 10 pages.
   How many pages did Avery read?

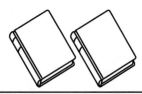

 **Reflect**

How did counting by tens help you solve problem 2?

_____

_____

Name _____

Count the objects. Write the number.

1.  _____

2.  _____

3.  _____

Solve. Show your mathematical thinking.

4. How many ducks are on this page?

 **Reflect**

How did counting help you solve problem 4?

_____

_____

Name _____

Count the objects. Write the number.

1. 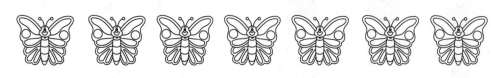 _____

2.  _____

3.  _____

Solve. Show your mathematical thinking.

4. Show three different ways to represent the number 6.

☀ **Reflect**

What do numbers represent?

_____

_____

Circle the set that is greater in each row.

1.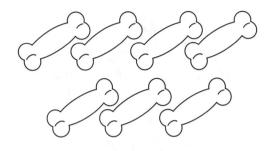

2.

Solve. Show your mathematical thinking.

3. Sara has 6 cookies. She wants to share them with 5 friends. Does Sara have enough cookies for everyone? How do you know?

✳ Reflect

How could drawing a diagram help you solve problem 3?

_____

_____

Name _____

Count the objects. Write the number.

1.  _____

2.  _____

3. 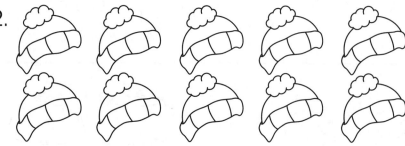 _____

Solve. Show your mathematical thinking.

4. Does the group of snowflakes below have *more* or *less* snowflakes than problem 3?

more   less

 Reflect

What strategy did you use to solve problem 4? Explain.

_____

_____

Name _____

Draw an equal set of different objects in each box.

1.

2.

3.

Solve. Show your mathematical thinking.

4. Graham and Olivia each took a handful of counting bears. Graham had more bears than Olivia. Show how many bears Graham might have and how many Olivia might have.

✷ **Reflect**

Explain another way Graham could have more bears than Olivia.

_____

_____

Compare. Circle the number that is less.

1.   9   6

2.   3   8

3.   2   5

Solve. Show your mathematical thinking.

4. Ben and Sam were rolling dice at their math station. Ben rolled a 5. Sam rolled a 🎲. Compare Ben's and Sam's rolls.

_____

_____

_____

_____

☀ Reflect

How did Ben and Sam know that their rolls were equal?

_____

_____

_____

_____

Name _____

Compare. Circle the number that is greater.

1.   5   4

2.   7   5

3.   1   10

Solve. Show your mathematical thinking.

4. Circle the number below that is the greatest.

| 1 | 2 | 3 | 4 | 5 | 6 | 7 | 8 | 9 | 10 |

✺ **Reflect**

How do you know that the circled number is the greatest?

_____

_____

_____

_____

_____

Name _____

Circle the set of numbers that are equal in each row.

1.   1, 10   10, 10   10, 0

2.   5, 4   9, 4   5, 5

3.   6, 6   9, 6   3, 8

Solve. Show your mathematical thinking.

4. Jose saw 7 butterflies. Jennifer saw 9 butterflies. Who saw fewer butterflies?

Reflect

How did you know who saw fewer butterflies?

_____

_____

_____

_____

Name _____

Solve.

1. How many books altogether? _____ 📖📖📖📖📓📓

2. How many birds are left? _____ 🐦🐦🐦🐦🐦

3. How many feet do you see? _____ 🐞🐞

Solve. Show your mathematical thinking.

4. Nine bees were near the beehive. Some flew into the hive. Now, there are only 5 bees. How many bees flew into the hive?

```



```

☀ Reflect

The bees flew away to where they could not be seen. How does this show subtraction?

_____

_____

_____

Name _____

Solve. Draw pictures to match.

1. 3 + 4 = _____

2. 5 + 6 = _____

3. 2 + 2 = _____

Solve. Show your mathematical thinking.

4. Bill has 1 red pencil. Zack has 7 yellow pencils. How many pencils do they have altogether?

 **Reflect**

Why is drawing pencils a good way to solve problem 4?

_____

_____

Name _____

Solve. Draw pictures to match.

1. 3 and 3 _____

2. 6 take away 4 _____

3. 10 take away 2 _____

Solve. Show your mathematical thinking.

4. Grace has 6 stuffed animals on her bed. She has 3 stuffed animals on the floor. How many stuffed animals does Grace have altogether?

✴ Reflect

Grace has 9 stuffed animals altogether. Three stuffed animals fall onto the floor. How do you know that 6 are left on the bed?

_____

_____

Name _____

Solve. Show your work with pictures or numbers.

1. John ate 3 pieces of fruit for lunch. He ate 1 banana and some strawberries. How many strawberries did John eat?

_____

2. There were 6 ants crawling on the blanket. Two bees landed on the blanket. How many bugs were on the blanket altogether?

_____

Solve. Show your mathematical thinking.

3. There were 7 students in the classroom. Four students were seated. The rest of the students were standing. Jamie said 2 students were standing. Was she right? How do you know?

_____

_____

_____

☀ Reflect

How did you solve problem 3?

_____

_____

_____

_____

Name _____

Color the domino that matches each number sentence.

1. 2 + 4 = 6

2. 6 + 0 = 6

3. 3 + 3 = 6

Solve. Show your mathematical thinking.

4. George and Lynn each picked up a domino. George said that both dominoes had the same number of dots. Lynn did not believe him. Was George right? How do you know?

George

Lynn

_____

Reflect

Retell George and Lynn's problem. What were they trying to find?

_____

_____

_____

_____

_____

Name _____

Solve.

1. Mom folded 7 shirts and put them in a pile. Ella bumped into the pile. Two shirts fell off. How many shirts were left in the pile?

_____

2. Dad was helping mom. He saw the 7 shirts. He brought 3 more to fold. How many shirts did mom have altogether?

_____

Solve. Show your mathematical thinking.

3. Darius had 8 socks. Some were blue, and some were red. How many were blue? How many were red?

```

```

✺ Reflect

In what different way could some socks be red and some socks be blue?

_____

_____

_____

Name _____

Solve.

1. There were 8 apples in the tree. Six apples fell to the ground. How many apples were left in the tree?

_____

2. James ate 2 chocolate muffins. Ryan ate 4 blueberry muffins. How many muffins did the boys eat altogether?

_____

Solve. Show your mathematical thinking.

3. Six cats were sleeping in the barn. Sam saw 2 wake up and go outside. How many cats were left in the barn?

```



```

☀ **Reflect**

How did you solve problem 3? What did you do first? Why?

_____

_____

_____

Name _____

Show two different ways to make each number.

1. 9

2. 6

3. 7

Solve. Show your mathematical thinking.

4. Javier grabbed 5 cubes out of the box. Some were yellow, and some were green. Show three different ways that some could be yellow and some could be green.

☀ **Reflect**

In what other way could some cubes be yellow and some cubes be green?

_____

_____

Name _____

Show three different ways to make 7.

1. [ ]

2. [ ]

3. [ ]

Solve. Show your mathematical thinking.

4. At the park, 9 children were playing. Some children were on the slide, and some children were on the swings. Show two different ways the children could be playing on the slide and the swings.

[ ]

☀ Reflect

Could all of the children be playing on the slide? Why or why not?

_____

_____

Name _____

Zoe made peanut butter sandwiches and cheese sandwiches for her friends.

Show two different combinations of sandwiches Zoe could make. Color the peanut butter sandwiches brown. Color the cheese sandwiches orange.

Write a number sentence about each picture.

1.   _____

2.   _____

Solve. Show your mathematical thinking.

3. Zoe forgot to make herself a sandwich. Now, she needs 9 sandwiches in all. More friends like peanut butter than cheese. Draw all of Zoe's sandwiches.

Write a number sentence about your picture. _____

☀ Reflect

Could Zoe make 5 of each sandwich? Why or why not?

_____

_____

Name _____

There are 5 frogs at the pond. Some frogs are in the water, and some frogs are on a log. Show the frogs in three different ways.

1.

2.

3.

Solve. Show your mathematical thinking.

4. If all 5 frogs hop into the pond, how many frogs will be left on the log?

![Reflect icon] **Reflect**

What would happen if 2 more frogs hopped into the pond?

_____

_____

Name _____

Fill in each ten frame to find out how many are needed to make 10.

1.

6 and _____ make 10

2.

5 and _____ make 10

3.

1 and _____ make 10

Solve. Show your mathematical thinking.

4. Use the ten frames to show two more ways to make 10.

_____ and _____ make 10   _____ and _____ make 10

⚡ **Reflect**

How do you know that there are more ways to make 10?

_____

_____

Name _____

Each basket can hold 10 apples. How many more apples are needed to fill each basket?

1. _____ more apples

   3 and _____ make 10

2. _____ more apples

   6 and _____ make 10

3. _____ more apples

   0 and _____ make 10

Solve. Show your mathematical thinking.

4. Emma found 6 apples on the ground. Her friends have baskets that are not full. Whom can she give all of her apples to?

_____

Gabe's Basket   David's Basket   Laura's Basket

★ **Reflect**

If Emma had found only 2 apples, whom could she have shared them with to fill a basket of 10?

_____

_____

Name _____

Each cloud can drop 10 raindrops. How many more raindrops can each cloud drop?

1. _____ more raindrops

10 and _____ make 10

2. _____ more raindrops

2 and _____ make 10

3. _____ more raindrops

7 and _____ make 10

Solve. Show your mathematical thinking.

4. Each box of crayons holds 10 crayons. Sydney was putting away the blue and yellow crayons. Color the crayons to show two ways Sydney could have put the crayons into each box.

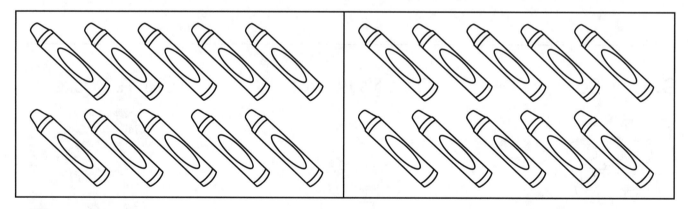

☀ Reflect

Why could Sydney not have put 6 blue and 6 yellow crayons into the same box?

_____

_____

Name _____

Each bowling ball can knock down 10 pins. How many more pins can each ball knock down?

1. _____ more pins

9 and _____ make 10

2. _____ more pins

3 and _____ make 10

3. _____ more pins

0 and _____ make 10

Solve. Show your mathematical thinking.

4. Show all of the ways to make 10.

0 and _____ make 10   _____ and _____ make 10

1 and _____ make 10   _____ and _____ make 10

2 and _____ make 10   _____ and _____ make 10

_____ and _____ make 10   _____ and _____ make 10

_____ and _____ make 10   _____ and _____ make 10

_____ and _____ make 10

☀ Reflect

What pattern do you notice in problem 4?

_____

Name _____

Solve.

1. 3 + 1 = _____

2. 5 + 0 = _____

3. 2 – 2 = _____

4. 4 – 3 = _____

5. 2 + 1 = _____

6. 1 – 1 = _____

Solve. Show your mathematical thinking.

7. Circle the picture that matches the number sentence.

1 + 4 = 5

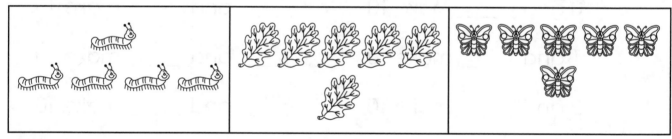

✺ **Reflect**

Which two pictures in problem 7 are almost the same? How do you know?

_____

_____

_____

Name _____

Solve.

1. 4 – 2 = _____

2. 2 + 1 = _____

3. 1 + 4 = _____

4. 3 – 3 = _____

5. 1 + 3 = _____

6. 5 – 0 = _____

Solve. Show your mathematical thinking.

7. Circle the number sentence that matches the picture.

   +

3 + 3 = 6   3 + 2 = 5   2 + 2 = 4

 Reflect

How does knowing the equation 3 + 2 = 5 help you solve 2 + 3 = 5?

_____

_____

_____

_____

_____

Name _____

Solve.

1. 1 + 2 = _____

2. 0 + 4 = _____

3. 2 + 3 = _____

4. 4 + 1 = _____

5. 2 + 2 = _____

6. 5 + 0 = _____

Solve. Show your mathematical thinking.

7. Color the cubes to show three different ways to make 5.

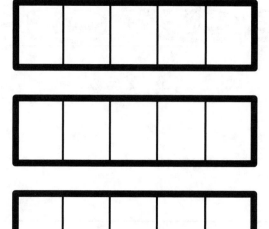

 **Reflect**

What math ideas helped you solve problem 7?

_____

_____

Name _____

Solve.

1. $1 - 0 =$ _____

2. $5 - 3 =$ _____

3. $4 - 2 =$ _____

4. $3 - 3 =$ _____

5. $5 - 1 =$ _____

6. $4 - 3 =$ _____

Solve. Show your mathematical thinking.

7. Write the subtraction problem for the picture.

```
┌─────────────────────────────────────────┐
│                                         │
│                                         │
│                                         │
│                                         │
└─────────────────────────────────────────┘
```

☀ Reflect

What strategies or tools are helpful when you subtract?

_____

_____

_____

Name _____

Count each ten frame and leftover ones. Write the number.

1.

_____

2.

_____

3.

_____

Solve. Show your mathematical thinking.

4. There are 10 crayons in the box. There are 4 crayons on the
   desk. How many crayons are there altogether?

✺ **Reflect**

What number sentence shows how many crayons were in the box
altogether?

_____

_____

Name _____

Each basket holds 10 kittens. Write the number of kittens in all.

1.   _____

2.   _____

3.   _____

Solve. Show your mathematical thinking.

4. Draw a picture to show the number sentence 10 + 2 = 12.

☀ **Reflect**

What do the digits 1 and 2 represent in the number 12?

_____

_____

Name _____

Show the numbers on the ten frames.

1. 16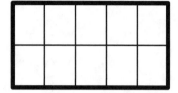

2. 19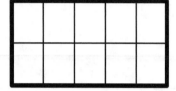

3. 11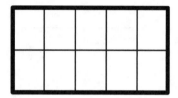

Solve. Show your mathematical thinking.

4. Eric picked 15 flowers for his mom. His mom's vase holds 10 flowers. How many flowers will be left out of the vase?

☀ Reflect

How would the strategy you used in problem 4 work if Eric had picked only 12 flowers?

_____

_____

Name _____

Choose one word below to describe each picture. Words may be used more than once.

| big | heavy | light | short | small | tall |

1. _____

2. _____

3. _____

4. _____

Solve. Show your mathematical thinking.

5. Ella is taller than her friend Mia. Draw a picture of Ella and Mia. Write each girl's name by her picture.

_____	_____

☀ **Reflect**

How did you know which girl was Ella and which girl was Mia?

_____

_____

Name _____

Choose one word below to describe each picture. Words may be used more than once.

big	heavy	light	short	small	tall

1. _____

2. _____

3. _____

4. _____

Solve. Show your mathematical thinking.

5. Describe the zebra. Use words from the word box above to help you.

_____

_____

☀ **Reflect**

The zookeeper has to feed the animals above. Which animal do you think will need more food than the others? Why?

_____

_____

Name _____

Choose one word below to describe each picture. Words may be used more than once.

| big | heavy | light | short | small | tall |

1. _____

2. _____

3. _____

4. _____

Solve. Show your mathematical thinking.

5. Draw a picture of your teacher. Describe your teacher. Use the words from the word box above to help you.

_____

_____

_____

☀ **Reflect**

Why are words such as *big, heavy, light, short, small,* or *tall* important for describing objects?

_____

_____

Name _____

Circle the larger object in each row.

1.

2.

3.

Solve. Show your mathematical thinking.

4. Circle the jar that will hold more marbles. How do you know?

_____

_____

✷ Reflect

How could you prove which jar is larger?

_____

_____

Name _____

Color the shorter object in each row.

1.

2.

3.

Solve. Show your mathematical thinking.

4. Dad has 2 garden hoses. How can he find out which hose is longer?

_____

_____

✹ **Reflect**

Why is it important to line up objects when trying to find out which one is longer?

_____

_____

Name _____

Color the heavier object in each row.

1.

2.

3.

Solve. Show your mathematical thinking.

4. Draw two different-sized apples. Circle the apple that would be lighter.

⬛ **Reflect**

How do you know which apple would be lighter?

_____

_____

Name _____

Draw a line to match each object to the correct category.

1.

 Animals

 Plants

Solve. Show your mathematical thinking.

2. Draw one more object for each category.

Animals	Plants

 Reflect

In what other way could you have sorted the objects above?

_____

_____

Name _____

Sort each animal into the correct category.

bear   dolphin   horse   sea horse   shark   tiger

Lives on Land	Lives in Water
1.	4.
2.	5.
3.	6.

Solve. Show your mathematical thinking.

7. Name animals that would fit into both categories.

_____

_____

 Reflect

Why is it important to know how things fit into categories?

_____

_____

_____

Name _____

Sort each number into the correct circle.

1.   8   12   15   3   1   11   4   18

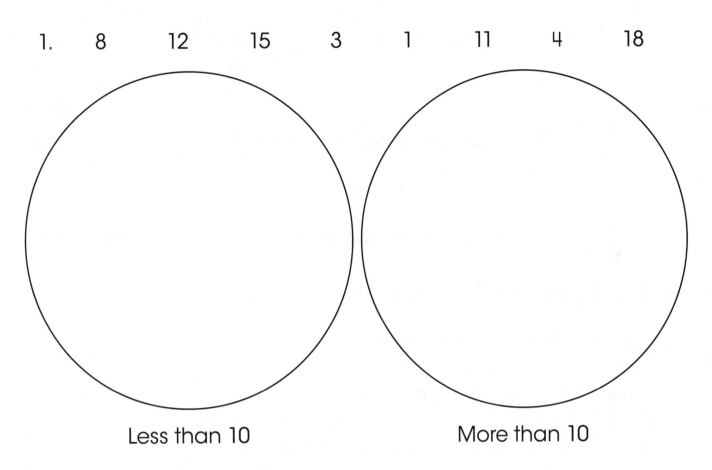

Less than 10   More than 10

Solve. Show your mathematical thinking.

2. Add two more numbers to each sorting circle. Draw a box around the numbers you added.

 **Reflect**

What other rule could you have used to sort the numbers?

_____

_____

_____

_____

Name _____

Look at each picture. Read each sentence. Circle *yes* or *no*.

1. The apple is **beside** the sandwich.   yes   no

2. The bear is **behind** the bow tie.   yes   no

3. The music note is **above** the horn.   yes   no

Solve. Show your mathematical thinking.

4. Draw 4 raindrops below the clouds.
   Draw 1 sun behind the clouds.
   Draw 1 bird beside the clouds.
   Draw 2 more clouds above the clouds.
   Draw 1 lightning bolt in front of the clouds.

☀ Reflect

Where are the raindrops in comparison to the sun in problem 4?

_____

_____

Name _____

Name each shape.

1. _____

2. _____

3. _____

Solve. Show your mathematical thinking.

4. How do you know this is a square?

_____

_____

_____

✳ Reflect

What other shapes have four sides?

_____

_____

Name _____

Find and name examples of each shape in your classroom.

1. square

_____

_____

2. triangle

_____

_____

3. rectangle

_____

_____

Solve. Show your mathematical thinking.

4. Circle the picture that shows two squares below a triangle.

Reflect

Why did you not circle the other pictures in problem 4?

_____

_____

Name _____

Name each shape.

circle	hexagon	square	triangle

1.  _____

2. _____

3. _____

4. ◯ _____

Solve. Show your mathematical thinking.

5. How do you know that both A and B are triangles?

A.   B.

_____

_____

✳ Reflect

What do you notice about triangles?

_____

_____

Name _____

Name each shape.

| cone | cube | cylinder | sphere |

1. _____

2. _____

3. _____

4. _____

Solve. Show your mathematical thinking.

5. Find and name three cubes in your classroom.

_____

_____

_____

☀ Reflect

How would you describe a cube?

_____

_____

_____

Count to tell how many of each shape are shown.

1. spheres _____

2. circles _____

3. cubes _____

4. squares _____

Solve. Show your mathematical thinking.

5. Kami says that circles and spheres are the same shape. Is Kami right? Why or why not?

_____

_____

_____

_____

☀ Reflect

Kami is still not sure. Name some examples of circles and spheres to help her.

_____

_____

_____

_____

Name _____

Color the flat shapes blue.
Color the solid shapes red.

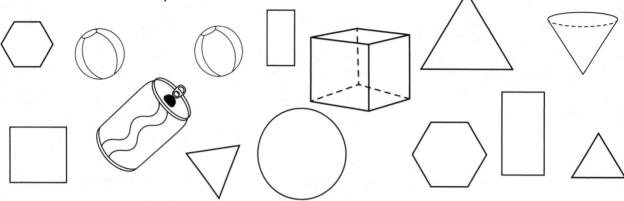

Solve. Show your mathematical thinking.

1. Jill sorted these shape names. Label the T-chart to tell how she sorted.

cube	rectangle
cylinder	circle
cone	square
sphere	triangle

☀ Reflect

Why are 3-dimensional shapes sometimes called solid shapes?

_____

_____

_____

Name _____

Name three flat shapes.

1. _____

2. _____

3. _____

Solve. Show your mathematical thinking.

4. Name five flat objects in your classroom. Tell the shape of each object.

Classroom Objects	Shapes

Reflect

Why are 2-dimensional shapes sometimes called flat shapes?

_____

_____

_____

_____

Name _____

Read each sentence. Circle *yes* or *no*.

1. A sphere is a flat shape.   yes   no

2. A square is the same shape as a cube.   yes   no

3. A cone is a solid shape.   yes   no

Solve. Show your mathematical thinking.

4. Cross out each shape name that is listed in the wrong category. Write it in the correct category.

Flat Shapes	Solid Shapes
hexagon	rectangle
cube	sphere
cone	square

✺ Reflect

Choose one shape name that you moved in problem 4. How did you know that it was in the wrong category?

_____

_____

_____

_____

Name _____

Fill in the blanks to describe each shape.

1. A square has _____ sides and _____ corners.

2. A circle has _____ sides and _____ corners.

3. A rectangle has _____ sides and _____ corners.

Solve. Show your mathematical thinking.

4. A square and a rectangle both have four sides and four corners. What makes them different shapes? Draw a square and a rectangle.

_____

_____

_____

_____

★ **Reflect**

How are squares and rectangles related?

_____

_____

_____

_____

Name _____

Fill in the blanks to describe each shape.

1. A cone has _____ faces and _____ vertices.

2. A cube has _____ faces and _____ vertices.

3. A sphere has _____ faces and _____ vertices.

Solve. Show your mathematical thinking.

4. Scott's little brother was wearing a party hat. Scott told his brother that he was wearing a cone. How did Scott know this was a cone?

_____

_____

✺ Reflect

How would you describe a cylinder?

_____

_____

_____

Name _____

Draw a line to match each flat shape to the solid shape that is most similar.

1. △

2. ▢

3. ◯

(solid shapes: sphere, cone, cube)

Solve. Show your mathematical thinking.

4. How are squares and cubes similar? How are they different?

_____

_____

_____

_____

☀ Reflect

How are a flat shape and a solid shape different?

_____

_____

_____

Draw each shape.

1. triangle

2. circle

3. rectangle

4. square

Solve. Show your mathematical thinking.

5. How can two squares be used to form a rectangle? Draw an example.

_____

_____

_____

☀ Reflect

Can any other shapes be used to form a rectangle? Why or why not?

_____

_____

_____

_____

Name _____

Draw each shape.

1. hexagon

2. cube

3. cone

Solve. Show your mathematical thinking.

4. Use the shapes you know to draw a picture. Label each shape.

✳ **Reflect**

What tools would be helpful when you draw shapes?

_____

_____

Name _____

Name the shape of each real-world object.

1. _____

2. _____

3. _____

Solve. Show your mathematical thinking.

4. Use the shapes you know to draw a robot. Label each shape.

```



```

✹ Reflect

What shape did you use the most? Why?

_____

_____

_____

Answer Key

Answers to some higher-level problems will vary but may include the answers provided. For all Reflect responses, accept all reasonable answers as long as students have proper evidence and support.

Page 5

1. 3; 2. 4; 3. 2; 4. 8 fish

Page 6

1. Students should trace the numbers 10, 20, 30, 40, 50, 60, 70, 80, 90, 100. 2. 20 pages

Page 7

1. 6; 2. 8; 3. 3; 4. 12 ducks

Page 8

1. 9; 2. 11; 3. 7; 4. Answers will vary but may include 6 tallies, 6 dots, or 5 + 1.

Page 9

1. 9; 2. 4; 3. 6; 4. The ten frame should be colored to show 6 dots of one color and 4 dots of another color.

Page 10

1. 11; 2. 4; 3. 8; 4. Check students' drawings.

Page 11

1. Students should circle the 7 bones. 2. Students should circle the 8 cats. 3. Check students' drawings.

Page 12

1. 4; 2; 10; 3. 9; 4. less

Page 13

1–3. Check students' drawings. 4. Answers will vary. Graham should have at least 1 more bear than Olivia.

Page 14

1. 6; 2. 3; 3. 2; 4. Ben and Sam rolled an equal amount.

Page 15

1. 5; 2. 7; 3. 10; 4. 10

Page 16

1. 10, 10; 2. 5, 5; 3. 6, 6; 4. Jose

Page 17

1. 6; 2. 3; 3. 8; 4. 4 bees

Page 18

1. 7; 2. 11; 3. 4; check students' drawings; 4. 8 pencils

Page 19

1. 6; 2. 2; 3. 8; check students' drawings; 4. 9 stuffed animals

Page 20

1. 2 strawberries; 2. 8 bugs; 3. No, three students were standing.

Page 21

1. 2. 3.
4. yes; Check students' reasoning.

Page 22

1. 5; 2. 10; 3. Answers will vary but should show a combination that totals 8.

Page 23

1. 2 apples; 2. 6 muffins; 3. 4 cats

Page 24

1–3. Check students' drawings. 4. Answers will vary but should show a combination that totals 5.

Page 25

1–3. Check students' drawings. 4. Answers will vary but should show two different combinations that total 9.

Page 26

1–2. Answers will vary but should show two different combinations and related number sentences that total 8. 3. Answers will vary but should show a combination and related number sentences that total 9.

Page 27

1–3. Check students' drawings. 4. 5 – 5 = 0 frogs; Check students' reasoning.

Page 28

1. 4; 2. 5; 3. 9; 4. Answers will vary but should show two different combinations that total 10.

Page 29

1. 7; 2. 4; 3. 10; 4. David

Page 30

1. 0; 2. 8; 3. 3; 4. Answers will vary but should show two different combinations that total 10.

Page 31

1. 1; 2. 7; 3. 10; 4. 10; 9; 8; 3, 7; 4, 6; 5, 5; 6, 4; 7, 3; 8, 2; 9, 1; 10, 0

Page 32

1. 4; 2. 5; 3. 0; 4. 1; 5. 3; 6. 0; 7. Students should circle the caterpillars.

Page 33

1. 2; 2. 3; 3. 5; 4. 0; 5. 4; 6. 5; 7. 3 + 2 = 5

Page 34

1. 3; 2. 4; 3. 5; 4. 5; 5. 4; 6. 5; 7. Answers will vary but should show three different combinations that total 5.

Page 35

1. 1; 2. 2; 3. 2; 4. 0; 5. 4; 6. 1; 7. 5 – 1 = 4

Page 36

1. 13; 2. 18; 3. 15; 4. 14 crayons

Page 37

1. 14; 2. 17; 3. 11; 4. Check students' drawings.

Page 38

1–3. Check students' drawings. 4. 5 flowers

Page 39

1. Answers will vary but may include small, short, or light. 2. Answers will vary but may include big, heavy, or tall. 3. Answers will vary but may include small or light. 4. Answers will vary but may include small, short,

Answer Key

or light. 5. Students' pictures should show Ella as taller than Mia as well as correct labeling.

Page 40

1. Answers will vary but may include big, tall, or heavy. 2. Answers will vary but may include big or heavy. 3. Answers will vary but may include small, short, or light. 4. Answers will vary but may include small or light. 5. Answers will vary.

Page 41

1. Answers will vary but may include small or light. 2. Answers will vary but may include small or heavy. 3. Answers will vary but may include small or light. 4. Answers will vary but may include small or light. 5. Answers will vary.

Page 42

1. The first ice-cream cone should be circled. 2. The second strawberry should be circled. 3. The second pumpkin should be circled. 4. The frst jar should be circled. Answers will vary.

Page 43

1. The second lizard should be colored. 2. The second dolphin should be colored. 3. The first snake should be colored 4. Answers will vary.

Page 44

1. The tractor should be colored. 2. The shark should be colored. 3. The watermelon should be colored. 4. Students should circle the smaller apple.

Page 45

1. Animals: goat, dolphin, hamster; Plants: carrot, tulip, tree; 2. Check students' drawings.

Page 46

1–3. horse, bear, tiger; 4–6. shark, sea horse, dolphin; 7. Answers will vary.

Page 47

1. Less than 10: 8, 3, 1. 4; More than 10: 12, 15, 11, 18; 2. Answers will vary.

Page 48

1. no; 2. yes; 3. yes; 4. Check students' drawings.

Page 49

1. triangle; 2. circle; 3. rectangle; 4. Answers will vary but may include that a square has four sides that are all the same size, has four corners, and is a flat figure.

Page 50

1–3. Answers will vary. 4. Students should circle the third picture.

Page 51

1. square; 2. hexagon; 3. triangle; 4. circle; 5. Answers will vary but may include the attributes of triangles or that moving or turning a triangle does not change its shape.

Page 52

1. cylinder; 2. cone; 3. sphere; 4. cube; 5. Answers will vary.

Page 53

1. 5; 2. 4; 3. 2; 4. 7; 5. George is not right. Answers will vary but may include differences such as one is a flat shape, one is a solid shape, or one rolls.

Page 54

Check students' coloring. 1. left column: Solid Shapes; right column: Flat Shapes

Page 55

1–4. Answers will vary.

Page 56

1. no; 2. no; 3. yes; 4. Cube, cone, rectangle, and square should be crossed out and moved to the other column.

Page 57

1. 4, 4; 2. 0, 0; 3. 4, 4; 4. Answers will vary but may include that a rectangle does not have to have all equal sides. Check students' drawings.

Page 58

1. 1, 1; 2. 6, 8; 3. 0, 0; 4. Answers will vary.

Page 59

1. triangle, cone; 2. square, cube; 3. circle, sphere; 4. Answers will vary but may include they are similar because they have right angles and the same flat shape, but they are different because one is flat and one is solid.

Page 60

1–4. Check students' drawings. 5. Answers will vary. Check students' drawings.

Page 61

1–3. Check students' drawings. 4. Check students' drawings and labels.

Page 62

1. cylinder; 2. sphere; 3. cube; 4. Check students' drawings and labels.